Materials and their Uses

By the end of this book you will know more about:

- Different materials.
- The properties of materials.
- The different ways in which materials are used.

You will:

- Plan and carry out fair test investigations.
- Use graphs and charts to present information.

Many different materials are used in school and at home.

Task 1

What's it made of?

1

- Look round your classroom and other parts of the school for objects made of different materials.
- How many different materials can you find?

- Use the chart on Task Sheet 1 to record what you find.

Plastic	Glass	Wood	Metal
ruler cup	window	door	door handle

Extra Challenge

- How many different materials can you find in your home?
- How many different objects can you find made of each material?

Here are some materials you might find:

Brick

Concrete

Fabric

Plastic

Paper

Wood

Glass

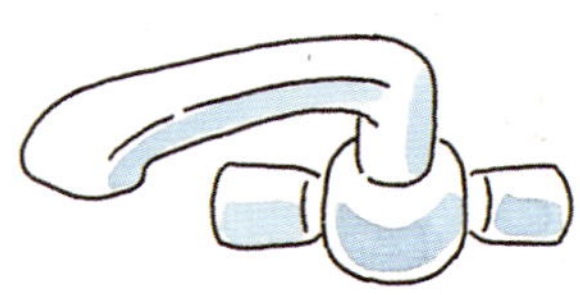

Metal

China

- Design your own table to record the materials you have found in your home.

Materials have different properties.

Task 2

Metal and its properties

- What do you know about metal?

- Which of the statements in the speech bubbles do you agree with?
- Write down the statements you agree with.
- What else do you know about metal?
- Add other statements of your own about the properties of metal.

Extra Challenge

- What do you know about plastic?

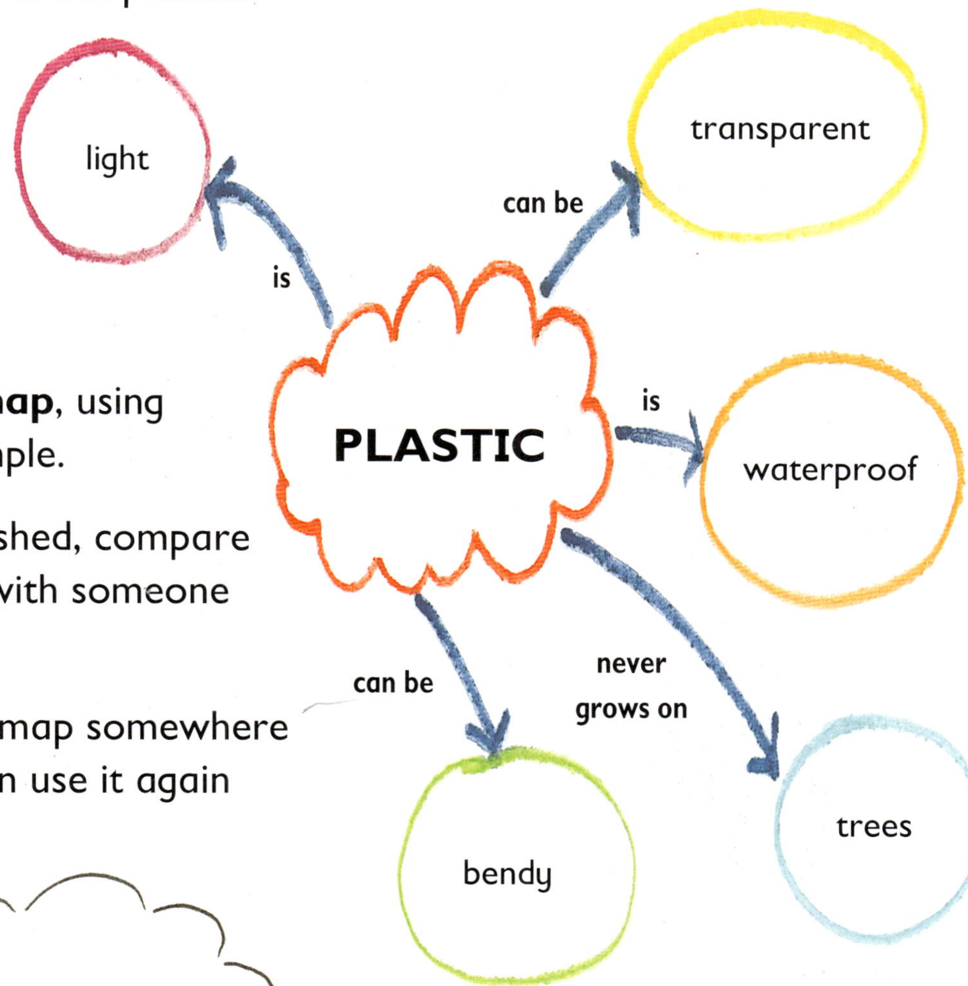

- Make a **concept map**, using this one as an example.
- When you have finished, compare your concept map with someone else's.
- Keep your concept map somewhere safe, so that you can use it again later on.

- What do you know about wood?
- Get into groups and brainstorm what you know about the properties of wood.
- Write down your ideas about wood in a list.

Different materials can be used to make the same object. Different objects can be made from the same material.

Task 3 *Same objects, different materials*

Here is a group of the same kind of object. Each object in the group is made of a different material.

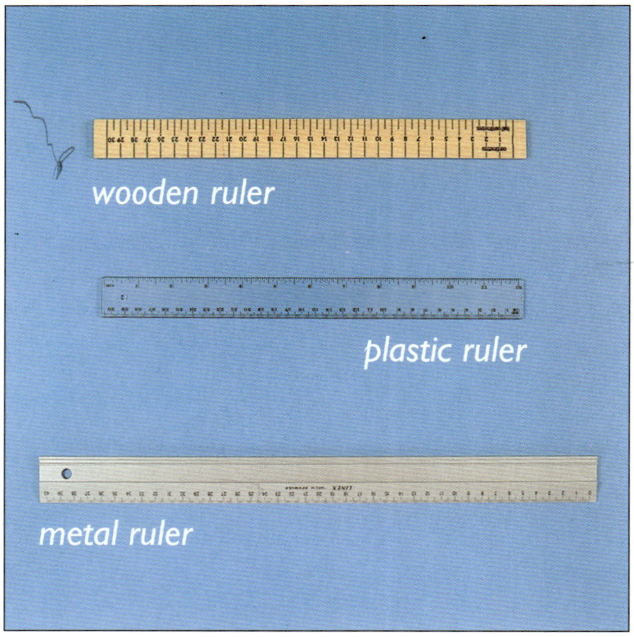

Group 1

- Look around your house or school for objects to make two groups of your own.

  All the objects in each group must be the same, but made of different materials.

- Which objects did you choose?

Group 2

Extra Challenge

- Now think about how many different objects you know that are made of the same material.

Plastic things

- Choose several different materials, such as plastic, glass, metal and wood.
- Make lists of all the objects you can think of made from each material.
- Make your lists as long as you can.

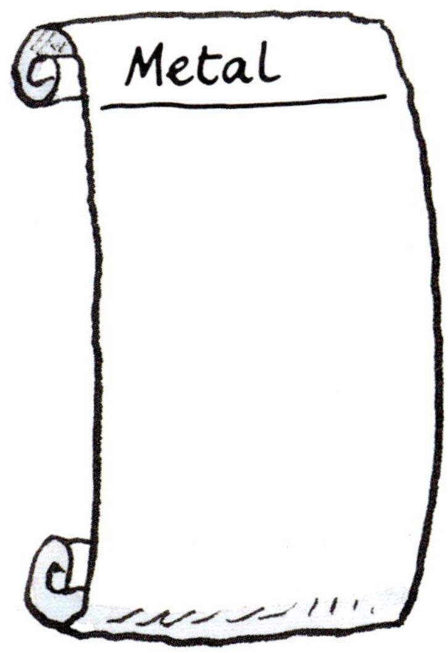

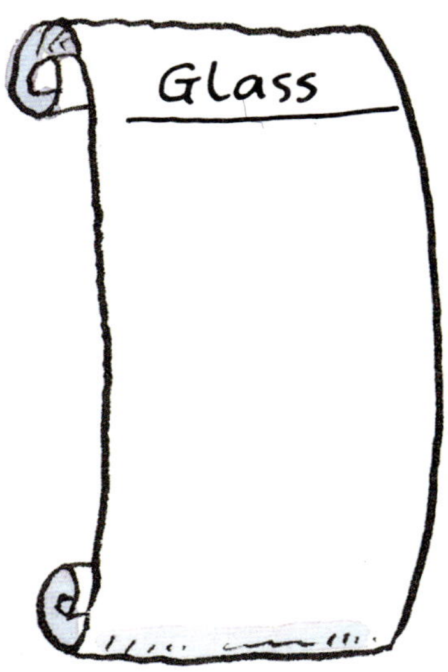

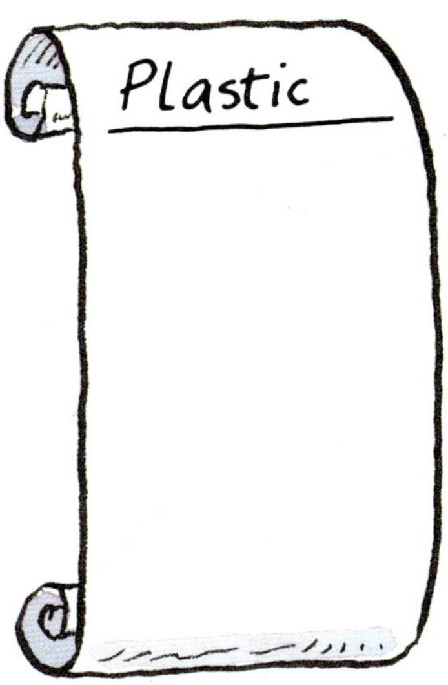

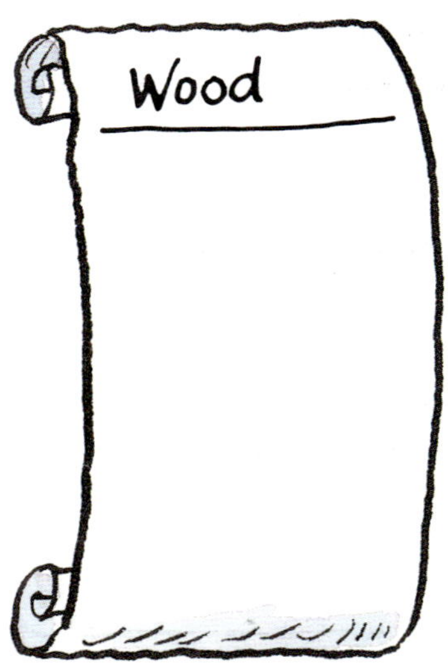

Task 4

What's the word?

2

Here are some words that people use to describe the properties of different materials:

- With a friend, think carefully about each word.
- Write down on Task Sheet 2 what you think each word means. This is called a **definition**.
- Look up the definition of each word in a dictionary.
- Check your definition - was it accurate? Do you need to change it?

Words to learn and use:
brick
ceramic
concrete
fabric
glass
material
metal
paper
plastic
wood

Task 5

Make a dictionary

- Make a properties of materials dictionary.
- Make it so that other people in your class will find it easy to use.

Here are some things to think about before you make your dictionary:

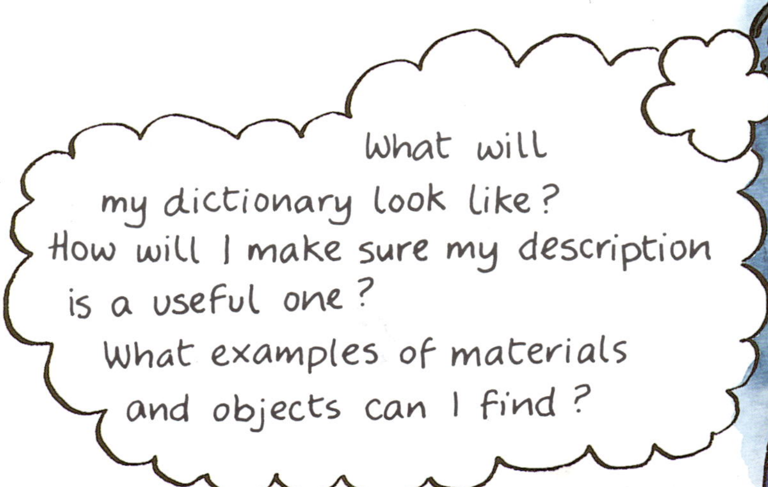

- How could you make your dictionary more interesting?
- Try some of these:
  - use a computer to present it in an attractive way.
  - illustrate it with pictures - perhaps clip art if you are using a computer.
  - include samples of materials.
  - highlight the most important words.

A material's properties make it suitable for particular jobs.

Task 6

Why use metal?

3

Metal is used to make many different objects.

Whenever metal is used, there are always good reasons for using it.

Here are some examples of metal objects, and the reasons why metal is used to make them.

METAL

Spoon

- It does not melt in hot liquids.
- It does not stain easily.
- It does not break easily.

Saucepan

- It allows heat to travel through the metal to the food.
- It does not melt on the cooker.

Nail

- It is strong.
- It can be made sharp.

Explain why the objects on Task Sheet 3 are made from the materials they are made from.

Task 7

That's just silly!

4

Newspaper wellies

Concrete pillow

Foam hammer

Imagine having a pair of wellington boots made from newspaper. What a silly idea!

Newspaper does not have the right properties for making wellingtons. It is not very strong and it is not at all waterproof. Your feet would get soaking wet and the boots would fall apart in no time at all.

The chart below gives you some silly suggestions and some sensible ones.

Object	Silly material	Sensible material	Why use the sensible material?
wellington	newspaper or plastic	rubber	rubber and plastic are waterproof and hard-wearing.
pillow	concrete	fabric	fabric is soft and washable.

Now add your own silly suggestions and then some sensible ones to the table on Task Sheet 4.

Plan and carry out fair tests to investigate different materials.

Task 8

Scientific Enquiry

Be a materials tester

Step-on Floors,
The Floor Covering Company,
Greater Walk Street,
Walkertown,
Walkshire

Dear Class,
We have just received a request for flooring for a new school hall. We would like your help to find out which material we should use for this job.
We are looking for a material that is hard-wearing and non-slip.
When you have finished your test, please send us a report with your conclusions.

Yours sincerely,

Claude Hopper

Managing Director

Small People's Clothing Company,
Little Lane,
Littleborough,
Smallshire

Dear Class
We would like to produce a new range of hard-wearing clothes for young children. Our designers need to know which fabrics are most likely to withstand the rough and tumble of toddlers playing and crawling.
Please test a number of fabrics for us and produce a report.

Yours sincerely,

Minnie Scule

Managing Director

- Choose one of these two letters and write a reply.
- How will you carry out your test to answer their question?
- What will you measure in your test?
- What equipment will you need?
- How will you make sure that it is a fair test?
- How will you record and present your results and conclusions to the company?

Extra Challenge
Writing your report

Before you write your report, think about:

Here are some ideas you might want to use in your report:

Use these sentence openers to help you write your report:

We decided to ...
Our plan was ...
We used ...
It was interesting that ...
We observed ...
The table showed that ...
Here you can see that the graph ...
Finally, our conclusion is that ...
So we recommend that ...

Task 9

The properties of paper

5

- Look at the different kinds of paper in the picture below.

YOU NEED:

different types of paper

- Make your own collection of different kinds of paper.
- Look at each type of paper very closely using a hand lens or microscope.
  What is it like?
  How is it different from or the same as the other types of paper?
- Use Task Sheet 5 to record the properties of each type of paper.

Type of paper	Use	Drawing of paper under microscope	Words to describe what you see	Words to describe the paper's texture

Plan and carry out a fair test to investigate the absorbency of paper.

YOU NEED:

different types of paper

Task 10

Scientific Enquiry

How absorbent is it?

6

- A class of children tested different kinds of paper to find out which paper absorbs water fastest.

- Use your ideas to plan and carry out your own investigation to find out which type of paper absorbs water fastest.
- How will you measure the results?
- How will you make sure that the test is fair?
- Before you begin your test, think about which of your papers will be best and why. Try to make a prediction of what will happen. Explain your choice of prediction.
- When you have finished, look at your results. Was your prediction correct?

Plan and carry out a fair test to investigate stretchy materials.

Task 11

Scientific Enquiry

How much do they stretch?

1

YOU NEED:

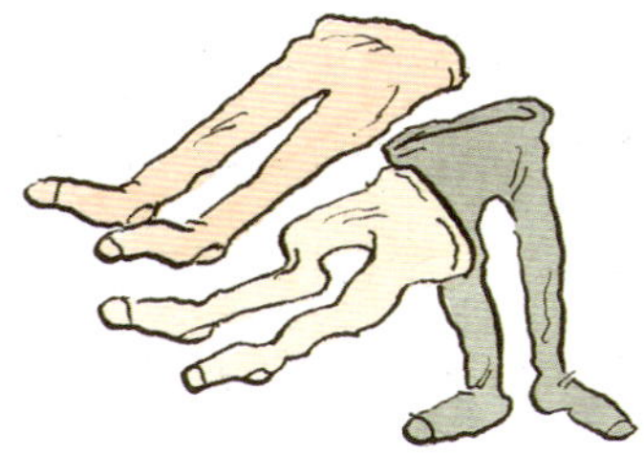

some different brands of tights

Nora Wrinkly loves her baggy tights.

They may not be fashionable, but she finds them so comfortable.

Sadly, the last time she bought a pair of tights they hardly stretched at all. She found them really awful to wear.

- Solve Nora Wrinkly's problem by finding out which tights are the stretchiest.

Think about these things before you start your test:

- What will you do to find out which tights are the stretchiest?

How will you make sure that you work safely?

- What will you measure?
- How will you make sure that your test is fair?
- How accurate will your measurements need to be?
- What kind of graph will you draw to show your results?

Words to learn and use:

bumpy
hand lens
microscope
rough
silky
smooth
sugar paper
texture
tissue paper

Nora Wrinkly has a fax machine.

Write a fax to send to Nora Wrinkly. Tell her about your investigations and the results.

Task 12

The Super Swimwear challenge

Imagine you are a fabric tester.
It is your job to test fabrics to find out which one should be used for a new range of bathing costumes for the Super Swimwear Company.

YOU NEED:

different fabrics

- What properties make a fabric suitable for swimwear?
- Make a collection of different fabrics.
- What will you do to test them?
- How will you record your results?
- When you have completed your tests, design and make a poster to advertise your Super Swimwear range.

YOU NEED:

different types of paper

Task 13 *Most absorbent nappy challenge*

- Disposable nappies can be made with two different materials – paper and plastic.

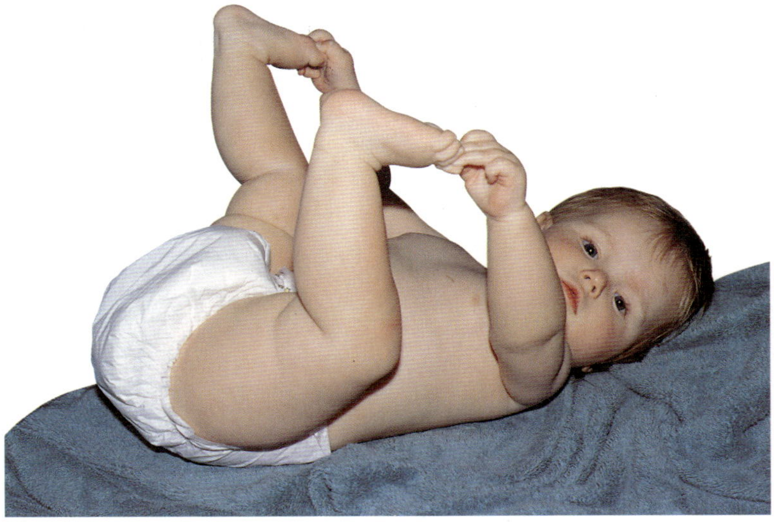

- The Never-Wet Nappy Company has had problems with its disposable nappies. The nappies are not absorbent enough and babies find them uncomfortable to wear.

- Your task is to design and make a disposable nappy.
- First you must test which kind of paper is best to use in the nappy.
- When you have finished, make an information leaflet about your new softer, more absorbent disposable nappy.

Checkpoint

Mystery materials grid

Hidden in this grid of letters are some words to do with materials and their properties.

- Look back through your work to remind yourself what you learnt about materials and their properties.
- Now find the hidden words.

The words may be horizontal, vertical or even diagonal - so keep your eyes peeled!

- What does each word mean?

A	M	F	J
E	A	B	S
F	T	L	R
L	E	K	V
E	R	N	U
X	I	G	X
I	A	Q	L
B	L	Z	C
L	W	O	D
E	A	B	W
B	D	J	C
M	G	E	Y
E	I	C	P
C	O	T	T

W	H	I	M	G	K	C	S
O	R	B	E	N	T	T	T
O	H	O	T	D	N	B	R
D	L	J	A	K	Z	A	E
Y	N	F	L	V	R	C	T
T	F	A	B	R	I	C	C
H	P	S	U	R	W	Y	H
A	R	J	O	U	I	M	Y
R	S	L	Q	S	X	C	I
D	T	S	H	P	V	Q	K
S	T	R	E	N	G	T	H
E	F	X	P	A	P	E	R
B	Z	I	G	A	D	A	G
O	N	M	S	B	O	R	F

Summary

Which of these do you know and which can you do?

- I know that many different materials are used in school and at home.
- I know some properties of different materials.
- I know that different materials can be used to make the same object and that different objects can be made from the same material.
- I know that a material's properties make it suitable for particular jobs.
- I can plan and carry out fair tests to investigate different materials.
- I can plan and carry out a fair test to investigate the absorbency of paper.
- I can plan and carry out a fair test to investigate stretchy materials.
- I can show my results in reports, graphs and tables.
- I can predict the results of my experiments and use the results to make conclusions.
- I can solve a problem about materials.

Complete your **Science Log** to show how well you know these and how well you can do them. Circle a face for each statement.

Glossary

absorbent

absorbent - able to soak up moisture.

ceramic - a material made of clay or mud baked in an oven called a kiln.

concrete - a mixture of cement, gravel and sand that sets hard and is used to make bridges, buildings and paths.

cotton - a light fabric made from a plant that grows in warm countries.

glass

elastic - regains its original shape after being stretched or squashed.

fabric - a material made from woven threads and used for clothes, furniture covers, towels and curtains.

flexible - can bend easily without breaking.

glass - a hard, transparent material made from sand that is used for window panes.

material - anything that can be used to make different objects.

metal - a strong, shiny material that comes from rocks in the ground.

plastic - a light, strong material made from chemicals in factories.

shiny - reflects light well and appears bright.

stretchy - can be pulled out longer or wider without breaking.

texture - the feel of a material.

concrete